MY ANIMAL KINGDOM

ALL ABOUT
LIONS

DeAGOSTINI

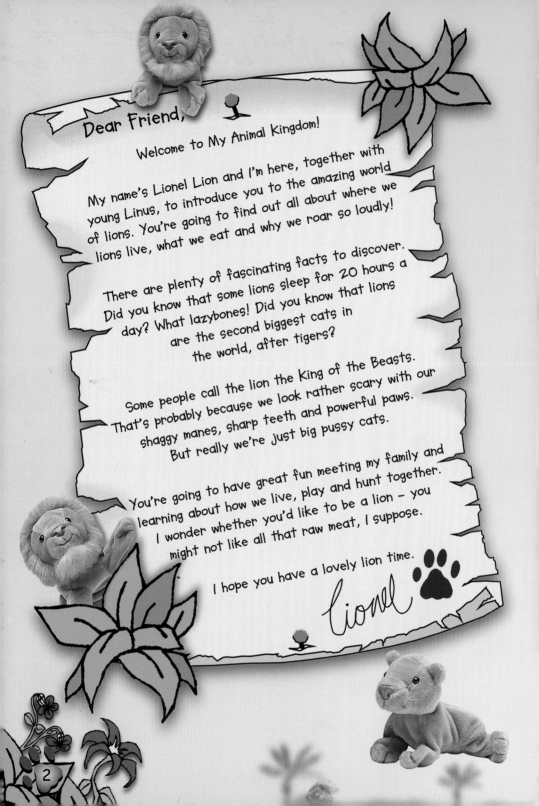

Dear Friend,

Welcome to My Animal Kingdom!

My name's Lionel Lion and I'm here, together with young Linus, to introduce you to the amazing world of lions. You're going to find out all about where we lions live, what we eat and why we roar so loudly!

There are plenty of fascinating facts to discover. Did you know that some lions sleep for 20 hours a day? What lazybones! Did you know that lions are the second biggest cats in the world, after tigers?

Some people call the lion the King of the Beasts. That's probably because we look rather scary with our shaggy manes, sharp teeth and powerful paws. But really we're just big pussy cats.

You're going to have great fun meeting my family and learning about how we live, play and hunt together. I wonder whether you'd like to be a lion – you might not like all that raw meat, I suppose.

I hope you have a lovely lion time.

Lionel

CONTENTS

Let's peek inside the pages!

LOOK AT ME

Lions are like pet cats but much, much bigger. An adult lion is as tall as you and a lot stronger - it could kill you with one swipe of its paw! In the wild, the lion hunts other animals for food. To catch them, it has to run very fast. It can run at 60 kilometres an hour - that's about the average speed of a car. But it can't keep up this speed for very long.

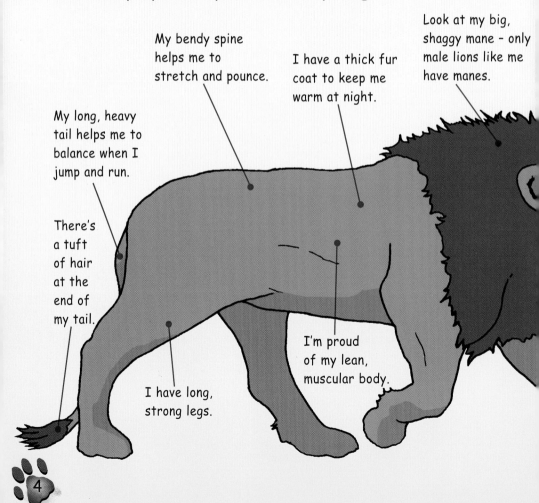

My bendy spine helps me to stretch and pounce.

I have a thick fur coat to keep me warm at night.

Look at my big, shaggy mane – only male lions like me have manes.

My long, heavy tail helps me to balance when I jump and run.

There's a tuft of hair at the end of my tail.

I'm proud of my lean, muscular body.

I have long, strong legs.

PAWS FOR THOUGHT

- A lion's paws are 12 cm wide – that's four times wider than a pet cat's.
- Thick pads on its paws help a lion to creep up on its prey without making a noise.
- A lion has four claws on each back paw and five on each front paw. Lions use the fifth claw like a thumb to help them grip things.

I have a big head and strong jaws for crunching up bones.

My big paws have strong, sharp claws for tearing up meat.

LION FACTS

LATIN NAME: Panthera leo

ANIMAL CLASS: mammal

ANIMAL ORDER: carnivore

ANIMAL FAMILY: Felidae

COLOUR: tan with white underbody

TOTAL LENGTH: 2.4–2.8 m

HEIGHT AT SHOULDER: 1 m

WEIGHT (MALE): 150–190 kg (about the same as 33 pet cats, or two adult humans)

RUNNING SPEED: Over short distances – 60 kilometres an hour – nearly one and a half times faster than a pet cat's top speed.

EATS: meat   **DRINKS:** water

LIVES: up to 30 years in captivity. In the wild, lionesses can live for 18 years and lions for 12 years.

All cats have bendy backs. That's how they run and jump so smoothly.

Lions have large, round heads and big brains. They have good eyesight and can even see well in the dark - about six times better than you can. They have a good sense of smell and keen hearing, too, which helps them to track down their food. They use their sharp, pointed front teeth to stab their prey and kill it instantly. Then they quickly gulp down their meal before another animal comes along to steal it!

I have a rounded head and a short face.

My whiskers help me to feel my way around in the dark.

With my powerful jaws and strong sharp teeth, I can break a bone with one bite.

OPEN WIDE

Adult lions have 30 teeth, and jaws that let them open their mouths extra wide. They need lots of room in their mouths because they don't chew up their food but swallow chunks of it whole.

Tearing teeth for ripping off pieces of meat

Crunching teeth

Long, sharp teeth for stabbing and killing prey

I have very good hearing.

Wow, what big teeth we've got!

My eyes are widely spaced, so I can see things to the side as well as in front of me.

WASH DAY

A lion's tongue is covered in lots of sharp spines. This lioness is using her tongue like a comb to tidy her cub's fur coat. But her tongue is so sharp it can scrape meat from bones too.

Most lions live in Africa, in areas of hot, dry grassland called savannah. There are only two seasons on the savannah – wet and dry. During the wet season, it rains almost every day and the grass grows as tall as a man. During the dry season, it doesn't rain at all and the grass dries up and turns yellow. The only trees that can grow on the savannah are ones that don't need much water, such as acacia and baobab trees.

WHERE IN THE WORLD?

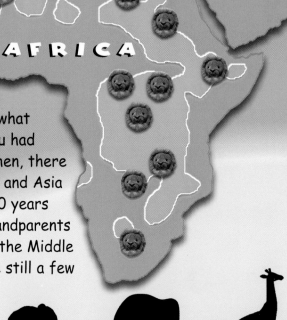

AFRICA

Imagine walking out of your house and seeing a lion strolling by! That's what you might have seen if you had lived 10,000 years ago. Then, there were lions all over Europe and Asia as well as Africa. Only 100 years ago – when your great-grandparents were alive – lions roamed the Middle East and India. There are still a few hundred lions in India.

People in different parts of Africa have different names for 'lion'. Here are a few:

- *simba* (the Swahili name in East Africa)
- *ngatia* or *muruthi* (the Kikuyu name in Kenya)
- *odum* (Nigeria)
- *ambess* (Ethiopia)

I'm hiding too!

LURKING LION

Lions have the purr—fect colouring to blend in with the grass of the savannah. It's very useful when they are looking for their lunch!

The savannah, where lots of lions live, is packed with animals. Spiders, scorpions and lizards feed on the billions of insects living in the grass. Birds swoop down to snatch up juicy bugs and gobble up the lizards and mice. Rodents, such as ground squirrels, scurry around too. Herds of antelope, wildebeest and zebra feed on the grass and shrubs. And let's not forget the fierce meat-eaters like leopards and hyenas.

STRIPED HIDE

Most animals on the savannah have stripes, spots or patches of colour on their coats. From a distance, these patterns look like shadows and help disguise the animals from predators.

I can see them, Dad!

FOOD FOR ALL

The animals on the savannah who eat plants are called grazers. Different grazers eat different plants so there's usually enough food for everyone. Zebras, wildebeest, warthogs and gazelles all graze on grass - but they eat different parts of the stem. Rhinos and antelopes feed on bushes and elephants eat the leaves on the trees. Only giraffes are tall enough to reach the tree-tops!

Hi! You're tall...

WHO LIVES ON THE SAVANNAH?

MEAT-EATERS
hyenas, leopards, cheetahs, baboons, lions and wild dogs

GRAZERS
gazelles, elephants, giraffes, springboks, antelopes, rhinoceros, warthogs, wildebeest, meerkats and zebras

BIRDS
eagles, bee-eaters, hornbills, ostriches, buzzards and vultures

REPTILES, RODENTS AND HARES
snakes, lizards, ground squirrels, mice and hares

CREEPY CRAWLIES
scorpions, beetles, termites, locusts, ants and spiders

Most cats like to keep themselves to themselves. Only lions live in groups. A group of lions is called a pride. There are about 15 lions in a pride – between 4 and 12 females, called lionesses, and up to 6 males. All the lionesses are related to each other – they are mothers and daughters, aunts and cousins. But the males come from different lion families. The pride doesn't stay together all the time. The lionesses divide up into groups of three or four and the males wander off by themselves. Each pride stays in its own territory, or area of land.

This is one of our most handsome cubs. He's big and strong already and likes to play with Linus.

This is a picture of my son, Linus, looking very cute – I'm really proud of him.

Me, pictured with Linus (on the right) and little cousin Lucy.

Lionesses Linda and Lena with their cubs, having a lie-down after lunch. We all look after each other's cubs, so there's always someone to help with the feeding, washing and babysitting.

13

It's not easy being a lion cub. If food runs short, the cubs are the first to go without a meal. There are also plenty of animals, such as hyenas, who see a lost cub as a tasty meal. So, when the lioness goes off on a hunt or climbs a tree to get some peace and quiet, she tries to hide her babies under a bush or in the long grass. Sometimes, she leaves one of the other lionesses to babysit while she is away.

BIG DADDY

Male lions love their own cubs and are very patient with them, but they don't like other lions' cubs! When a new male joins a pride, he often attacks the cubs already living in the group and starts his own family – lion life is tough!

Be careful Mummy!

QUICK LIFT
A cub has a fold of skin on the back of its neck, just like a kitten. A lioness picks up her cub by holding on to this – it doesn't hurt the baby a bit!

BABY FILE

BIRTH

A lioness leaves the pride to have her babies. She has between two and five cubs at a time. Each is about the size of a pet cat when it is born. Cubs can't see well at first and Mum does everything for them. After 10 days they start to walk, but they're not very steady on their paws. After a few weeks, Mum introduces them to the pride.

THREE MONTHS

Lion cubs are born with a spotty coat, which helps to camouflage them. They lose their spots by the time they are three months old. Their pink noses start to turn black and they get their first taste of meat. They stop drinking milk when they are eight months old.

ONE YEAR

Cubs learn to hunt when they are a year old. By then they are the size of a big dog. At two years old, the males have manes. At three years old, the cubs are fully grown.

Female lion cubs usually stay with the pride forever. Male lions leave when they are about three years old and roam around looking for a new pride to join. Sometimes they join other single males and look for a pride together. When they find one they like, they threaten the older males in it. They also spray their urine around the area of the land they want to take over - this is how lions mark their territory. Sometimes the old lions give up and leave the pride.

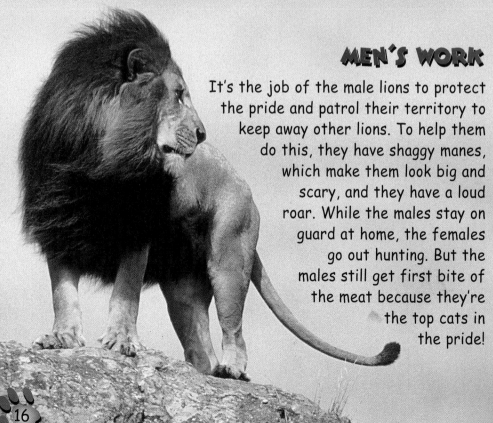

MEN'S WORK

It's the job of the male lions to protect the pride and patrol their territory to keep away other lions. To help them do this, they have shaggy manes, which make them look big and scary, and they have a loud roar. While the males stay on guard at home, the females go out hunting. But the males still get first bite of the meat because they're the top cats in the pride!

ROAR FACTS

Every morning and evening, the male lion goes out into his territory to roar. The noise is so loud it can be heard a very long way away. He roars to let any lions nearby know who's in charge!

That big roar sounds very scary...

WATCH OUT!

Even when they're drinking, lions are on the look-out for trouble – or perhaps a tasty snack!

WHAT I EAT

Lionesses are the main hunters in the lion family. They go out early in the morning or at night to look for animals to eat. When a lioness has spotted her dinner, she quietly creeps up on it. When she is about 20 metres away – about the length of five cars – she breaks into a run. She pounces on her prey, killing it with one swipe of her paw or a bite to the neck.

SHARING THE KILL

When a lioness has made her kill, she fetches the other lions. A big kill, such as a wildebeest or a big zebra, can feed the whole pride and there'll be no need to hunt for a few days.

TEAMWORK

A group of lionesses work together to catch big animals, such as zebra. Some of the lionesses hide in the long grass near the herd. Others sneak around the side of the herd and get behind them. Suddenly they leap out at the zebra and scare them towards the other lionesses.

lions

lions

prey

lions

PLAYTIME

Just like kittens, lion cubs practise their hunting skills by play-fighting with their brothers, sisters and cousins. They chase and pounce on each other. As they get older, play gets rougher. Lions start hunting for real when they are about two years old, but pet cats can hunt when they are only six months old.

MEATY MENU

TOP FIVE LION FAVOURITES:
- wildebeest
- gazelles
- buffalo
- warthogs
- hartebeest

ALSO GOOD TO EAT:
- zebras
- young giraffes
- young hippos
- young rhinos

QUICK SNACKS:
- snakes
- hares
- squirrels
- lizards
- birds

NO FRIEND OF MINE!

Lions don't have many animal enemies. But sometimes the weather gets the better of them. If there is a drought and the savannah grass dries up, the animals that eat the grass leave to look for food elsewhere. This means that there are fewer animals for the lions to hunt – they may even have to eat animals that have already died. Vultures circle overhead and packs of wild dogs and hyenas creep around hoping to steal the lions' food.

SNEAK THIEF!

Hyenas have crooked legs, mean faces and they smell horrible. Their coats are rough and look dirty. Their cry sounds like a nasty laugh, so they are called 'laughing hyenas'. Hyenas are scavengers – they feed on dead animals and anything they can steal. They like to annoy lions and even challenge them to fights. The lions chase them away. Lions can also get their own back by stealing the hyenas' dinner!

DANGER OVERHEAD!

As soon as the lions make a kill, flocks of vultures appear in the sky. They swoop down and try to steal some scraps from the lions.

Buzz off! You won't get any of our dinner.

PEOPLE POWER

A lion's most dangerous enemies are people. We have been killing lions for thousands of years and now there are only about 50,000 lions left in Africa and a few hundred in Asia. People hunt lions as a sport – lion hunting is still allowed in some African countries. People also kill lions because they are scared the lions will attack their families and their farm animals.

6:00 AM Sunrise. I woke up and wandered off for my morning's roar. Then I went back to sleep.

7:00 AM Woken up by Linus. Had a yawn and a stretch and went back to sleep.

8:00 AM Played with the cubs. Lisa, the youngest, kept biting my tail. Never mind, she'll make a good hunter some day.

9:00 AM The cubs settled down to a milky meal from their mum, so I got a bit of peace and quiet.

10:00 AM Time for a nap under a shady acacia tree. This is when it starts to get very hot out here on the savannah. I don't usually move from here until it cools down later in the day.

12 NOON The hottest part of the day. It's very quiet – all sensible animals are having a rest. I sat up in my favourite tree and had a snooze.

5:00 PM Took a walk down to the waterhole for a drink. The lionesses say this is a good spot to go hunting.

6:00 PM Sunset. It gets dark very quickly here. Luckily we lions have very good eyesight in the dark so we can still find our way around.

:00 PM The lionesses started to plan their night's hunting. I don't join in. My job is to patrol our territory while they're away. I don't want any other male lions coming near my pride!

8:00 PM Went to the top of the hill and had a good roar. That should warn off any of my rival lions.

9:00 PM The lionesses got back and took us to their kill. They were lucky tonight and caught a zebra without too much trouble. I tucked in first, then the lionesses had their share. The cubs had to wait for the grown-ups to finish.

9:30 PM Chased off a pack of hyenas who were lurking nearby. They wanted to grab the rest of our meal, but we scared them away.

10:00 PM The lionesses were tired from the hunt, so we all settled down for the night. I'll be up first in the morning to get the day started with a loud roar!

Lionel

23

Lions belong to the cat family. All cats are alike in certain ways. They all have sharp teeth and like to eat meat. They all have good eyesight, hearing and sense of smell. And they can all move quickly. Lions, tigers, jaguars, leopards and snow leopards are known as big cats. All the other wild cats and pet cats are known as small cats. The main difference between big and small cats is that the big ones roar.

NAME GAME

This wild cat lives in America. When people from Europe first saw it, they thought it was a lion that had lost its mane, so they called it the mountain lion. It's also known as a puma, cougar, catamount (short for cat of the mountain), mountain screamer, Indian devil and purple feather!

CHEETAH CHASER

Lions are called leaping cats - they sneak up on their prey and then pounce. Cheetahs are cats too, but they are called running cats. Cheetahs can run fast enough to chase after animals like zebras and catch them. In fact cheetahs can run faster than any other animal on land over short distances. They can sprint at a speed of 100 kilometres per hour!

AFRICAN WILD CATS

Lions aren't the only cats in Africa. Here are a few more:

- leopards
- cheetahs
- servals
- African wild cats
- caracals
- African golden cats
- black-footed cats
- sand cats

DID YOU KNOW?

Sea-lions are definitely not lions. But they are like big cats in some ways. Sea-lions eat meat and have hairy coats and whiskers. They also roar. Some types of male sea-lion even have manes!

The lion is often called the King of the Beasts. Most people and animals are scared of him. Lions have few enemies except for humans with guns. A male lion strides around as if he is the king of the whole savannah. Perhaps that's why there are so many stories about lions and why so many kings have chosen the lion as their symbol. Some of the great kings of Ancient Egypt, called pharaohs, even kept lions as pets!

LONDON LIONS

Artists and sculptors love drawing lions because they are so beautiful. A man called Edwin Landseer made these bronze statues of lions for Trafalgar Square in London. Millions of years ago, during the Ice Age, real lions lived at just this spot! That was long before the city was built.

What's that on his head?

- If your birthday falls between 22 July and 23 August (like Linus'), then your star sign is Leo. Leos are supposed to be fierce, loud and proud – just like real lions!
- The word lionize means to treat people as if they are very important.
- Leonine describes a person who is brave.

GONE WILD

Hundreds of years ago, hunters brought back strange animals from distant lands for everyone to see. Some rich men started their own zoos full of amazing animals. At first, people kept wild animals in small cages and made them do tricks. Today, big animals such as lions live in zoos and safari parks, where they have plenty of space to roam. But the best place to see lions is in the wild, in the game reserves of Africa.

This picture is one of my favourite holiday snaps.

WHAT DOES IT MEAN?

CAMOUFLAGE
This is a way of making things hard to see. An animal is camouflaged when the colour of its coat blends in with the trees or grass or snow it lives in.

CAPTIVITY
Another word for keeping a person or animal prisoner.

CARNIVORE
A meat-eater. All cats are carnivores.

DROUGHT
A spell of very dry weather when it doesn't rain for a very long time. Rivers dry up and the grass turns brown and dies.

GAME RESERVE
Game is another name for wild animals. A game reserve is a huge safari park where animals can live as they do in the wild, but they are looked after and protected.

GAZELLE
A kind of deer found in Africa. Antelopes are also a kind of deer.

PREDATORS
Animals that hunt other animals. Lions hunt zebras – zebras are their prey.

SAFARI
A trip to see and photograph wild animals. People once went on safari to hunt and shoot animals.

SCAVENGER
An animal that feeds on dead animals and other food that it finds lying around. Sometimes it steals from other animals.